# Beginner Ukulele Lessons for Kids

## Book with Online Video and Audio Access

### By
### Jay Wamsted

For Online Video & Audio Access, go to this address on the internet:

cvls.com/extras/kidsuke

## About the Author

Jay Wamsted teaches high school math in southwest Atlanta. He has been playing ukulele for over thirty years—sometimes in bands and sometimes alone. He holds a Ph.D. in education from Georgia State University and his published writing can be found both online and in various journals and magazines. In addition to teaching math, he has taught private music lessons; currently he is working with his own children on these very arrangements. Several of his original piano compositions can be streamed at Amazon Play, Apple Music, Spotify, and elsewhere.

## Watch & Learn Products Really Work

Over thirty years ago, Watch & Learn revolutionized instructional music courses by developing well thought out, step-by-step methods. These courses were tested for effectiveness on beginners before publication. These lessons have continued to improve and evolve into the Watch & Learn system that continues to set the standard of music instruction today. This has resulted in sales of more than three million products since 1979.

## About this Course

This course was designed for elementary school-aged children (5 years and up) with an emphasis on getting the student to play real music as quickly as possible. Our method is unique because of two basic concepts. First, we teach songs that many kids will already know. This avoids the student becoming overwhelmed by learning rhythm notation. Secondly, the chord shapes and strum patterns taught are intentionally very simple. This allows the student to have early success and get interested in playing the ukulele without getting overly frustrated and giving up.

It's important for the student to know that everyone learns at a different speed. Younger children may require more guidance to work through the book. It's also important for adults to remember to encourage the student and be proud of any progress that is made.

## Course Material

In addition to this book, you also have access to video instruction that covers all of the songs taught in the book. This is an important tool for helping the student play in time and with proper form.

We've also included access to audio tracks for each song. These can be downloaded and used to practice away from a screen.

cvls.com/extras/kidsuke

If you ever need any assistance accessing or using these materials, please send an email to sales@cvls.com. The tracks feature piano and ukulele by Jay Wamsted. The tracks were recorded by Toby Ruckert at uTOBYa Studio.

# Table of Contents

# Section 1
# Getting Started

For Online Video & Audio Access, go to this address on the internet:

cvls.com/extras/kidsuke

# The Ukulele

There are four main types of ukuleles as shown by the photos below. This course will work with a Soprano, Concert, or Tenor ukulele. The strings of these ukuleles are tuned G C E A.

Baritone ukuleles are larger and tuned differently. This course will not teach you how to play baritone ukulele.

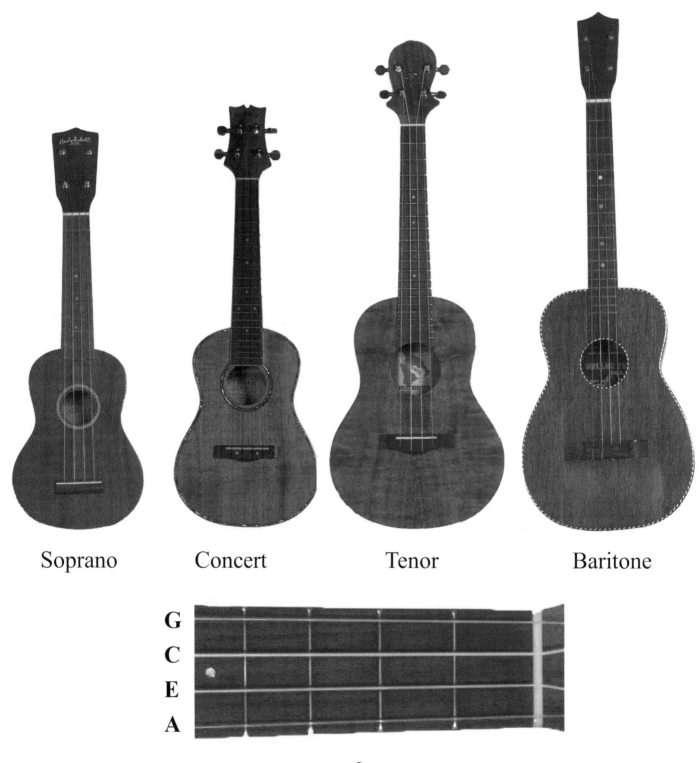

Soprano       Concert       Tenor       Baritone

# Parts of the Ukulele

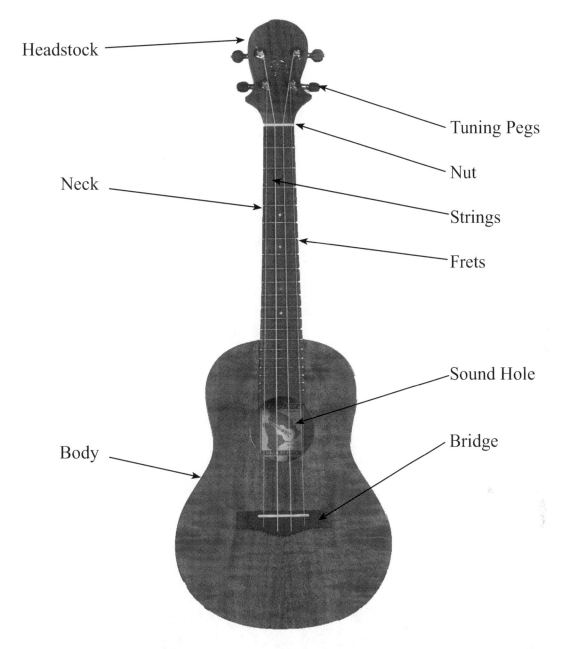

- There are three main sections of the ukulele: the headstock, the neck, and the body.
- The tuning keys are used to tighten and loosen the strings. This allows you to tune each string to the proper note.
- The nut helps hold the strings in place
- When you make the string vibrate with your finger or by striking it with a pick, you create sound.
- The frets are metal bars on the neck of the ukulele. When you play a string and hold the string against a fret, it creates a note.
- The sound hole is where the sound of the strings becomes louder.
- The bridge holds the strings in place just like the nut does at the other end of the neck.

# Seated Position

When you first start playing ukulele, it's easiest to use a seated position. You want to use a basic and comfortable chair that doesn't have arms on either side. You also want the height of the seat to allow your upper leg to be at an even position with your knee. This provides a good spot to rest your ukulele.

# Right Hand

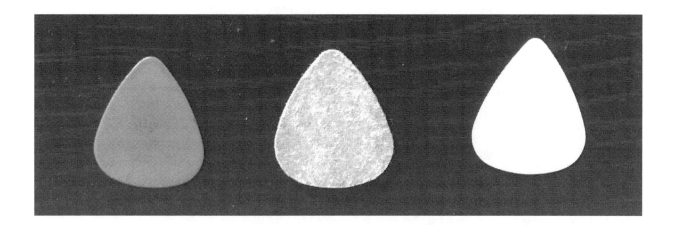

The most common way to play a ukulele to use a pick or plectrum. This is typically a triangle shaped piece of plastic that allows you to strike the strings and create a louder volume.

In the beginning, you may want to try using a thin or low gauge pick. They are a little bit easier to play with. You may also find that using a felt ukulele pick is easier to hold and doesn't play too loudly.

Don't have a pick? No problem. You can always use your thumb to strum the strings.

The most common way to hold the pick is between the thumb and index finger. First, you want to curl your index finger. With your left hand, place the pick on top of your index finger, then place your thumb on top of the pick with enough force to hold it in place.

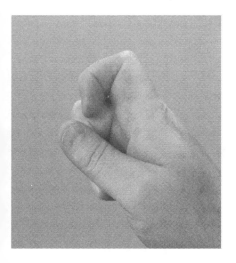  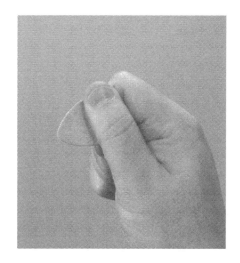

# Strumming

Use the pick to brush over the strings. When we play a few strings at the same time, we call it strumming.

Now try to play each string one at a time starting from the string closest to the ceiling. This is called the 4th string and plays the note G, 3rd string is a C, 2nd string is an E, and the first is an A.

Did your strings sound different than mine? It might be because your ukulele is out of tune. Your ukulele is probably made of wood and has strings, tuning pegs, nuts, and the bridge holding everything in place. Unfortunately, these different parts move over time or just because the temperature changes. When this happens, we have to make sure our strings are playing those notes (G, C, E, A) correctly. This process is called tuning.

# Tuning the Ukulele

The most common way to tune your ukulele is with either an electronic tuner or a tuning app. Luckily, most of these work the same way. If you play the 4th string (G), you may see an G show up on the screen. If the note your string is playing is too low or flat, you might see an F or F$\sharp$. You will need to tighten your string a little until you see the G show up in the middle. If the note played by your 4th string is too high, you may see A$\flat$ or A. This means you need to loosen your string a little.

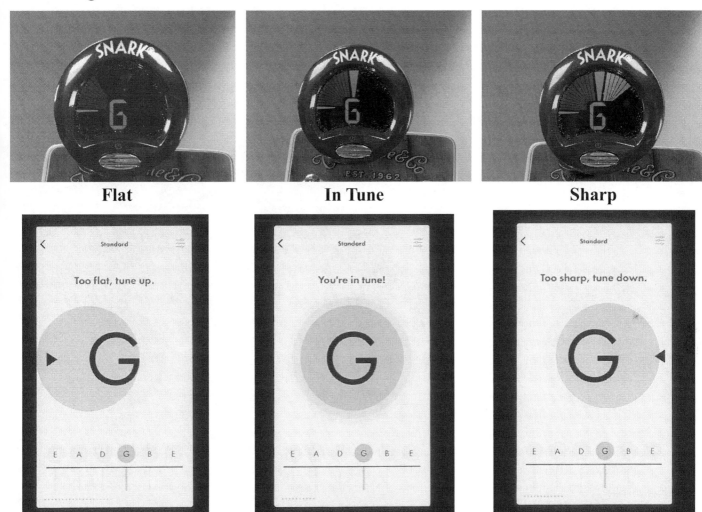

| Flat | In Tune | Sharp |

We then need to repeat this process for all four strings until they are playing the correct note. It's important that you tune your ukulele at the start of each practice session. Playing an out of tune ukulele is like baking a cake with the wrong ingredients. No matter how hard you try, it won't end up tasting very good. Even famous uke players would sound bad if they play out of tune ukuleles.

# Left Hand

We can use our left hand to make the ukulele play lots of different notes. Let's look at how that works.

We start by putting our left hand thumb on the back of the ukulele neck. Most uke players put their thumb in the middle of the curve of the neck. If you have a longer thumb, you may place it higher, and if your hand is smaller, you may need to place it lower.

## Thumb Position

You will see different players use different thumb positions, but we'll use this position because it allows you to play all of the chords without having to change your thumb position (Figure A).

The pad of your left thumb should be positioned on the center of the back of the ukulele neck. This will be our core position (Figure B).

 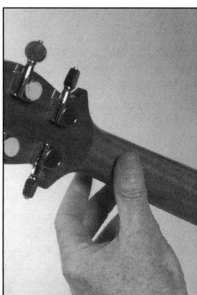

**Figure A**    **Figure B**

## Wrist Position

The wrist should be below the ukulele neck in a comfortable position. Don't strain your wrist to one side or the other (Figure C).

**Figure C**

# The G Chord

When we play several notes at the same time, it's called a chord. Let's learn our first chord.

When you learn chords, you'll be told how to play them by using a chord diagram. It looks like the neck of the ukulele has been rotated up-right and you're looking directly at it.

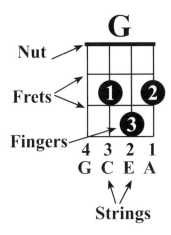

This is our first chord, G. The diagram shows you which frets and strings to place your fingers on. Our left hand is numbered 1 2 3 4. So the number 1 shows us that we're putting our pointer finger on the 2nd fret of the 3rd string. The number 2 shows us that we're putting our middle finger on the 2nd fret of the 1st string. The number 3 shows us we're putting our ring finger on the 3rd fret of the 2nd string.

The fingers are numbered as in the diagram to the right.

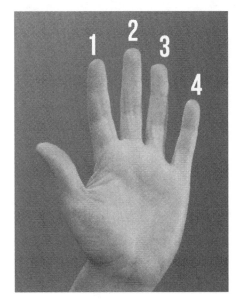

# The Strum

With our right hand, we're going to play strings 4, 3, 2, and 1 at the same time with a strum.

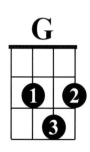

Now, let's play the G chord. Brush over the strings with your pick from the 4th string down towards the floor. Play the strum so that it sounds like all of the strings are being played at the same time. If you can hear each individual string as you strum down, then you're playing it too slowly.

Count out loud, 1 2 3 4. Try to strum down each time you say a number. When we strum down, you will see the following symbol in our music (/).

Watch and listen to the video instruction to make sure you're playing correctly. You can access the video by going to this address on the internet:

cvls.com/extras/kidsuke

14

# G Chord Song

Now let's play a song using the G chord.

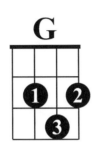

## G Chord Song

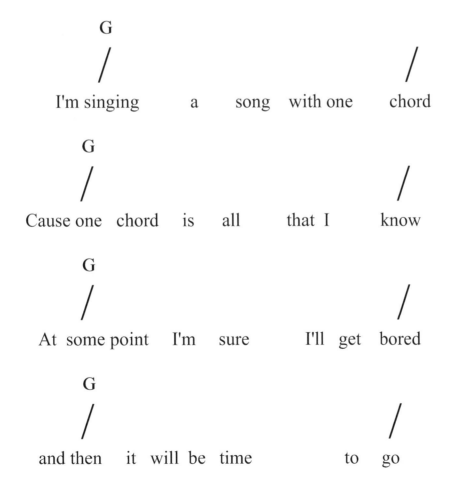

G

I'm singing     a    song   with one    chord

G

Cause one   chord   is    all     that I     know

G

At   some point    I'm    sure     I'll   get   bored

G

and then    it   will   be   time      to    go

15

# C Chord Song

Let's try a new chord, C. This time we're going to use one finger to play the chord. We'll place our 3rd finger on the 3rd fret of the 1st string.

Strum down from the 4th string. Now try playing each string one at a time. Can you hear each note clearly? You may need to arch your fingers more so that they are vertical enough not to touch another string. Also check your finger positions with the frets. Are you in the right spot?

Now play a song using the C chord.

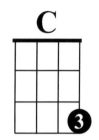

# C Chord Song

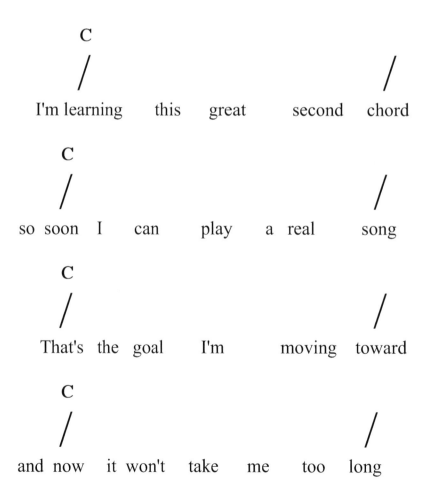

C
/                                    /
I'm learning    this   great    second   chord

C
/                                    /
so soon  I   can    play   a real    song

C
/                                    /
That's  the  goal   I'm      moving  toward

C
/                                    /
and now  it won't  take  me   too  long

# Changing Chords

We now know how to play two different chords. Before we can start our first real song, we need to work on switching between these chords.

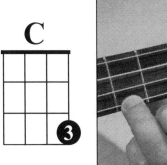  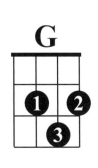 

When you first start learning and switching chords, it's going to take your fingers a little while to get in the correct spot. Over time as you practice, your fingers will start moving to the right positions quicker and quicker.

In our first song, we're going to switch from C to G and back and forth. So try making a C chord, play one strum for a count of (1-2-3-4) and then switching your hands to G and play a strum for a count of 1-2-3-4.

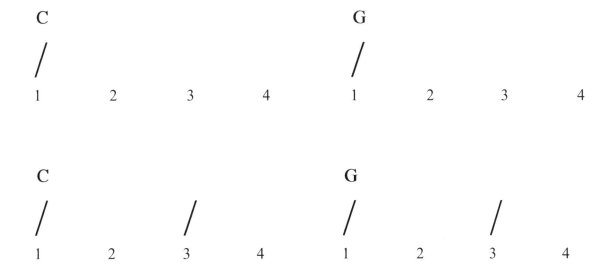

# Practice Tips

- Don't try to practice for an hour at a time. Try practicing for ten to twenty minutes once or twice a day.

- Stop if your fingers start to hurt.

- Tune your ukulele at the start of each practice session.

- First, watch the video for each song so you can see where your fingers should go and listen to the song.

- Second, practice playing the song with the book as slowly as you need to.

- Once you feel comfortable, try playing along with the video.

- Relax - if you're getting frustrated, try taking a break and coming back to it later. Learning the ukulele is supposed to be a fun experience, so enjoy yourself.

- It's ok if you make a mistake while playing a song. You may have to practice the song many times before your fingers remember what to do.

- If some of the notes don't sound right, you may need to arch your fingers more. The more vertical your fingers are, the less likely they are to touch another string.

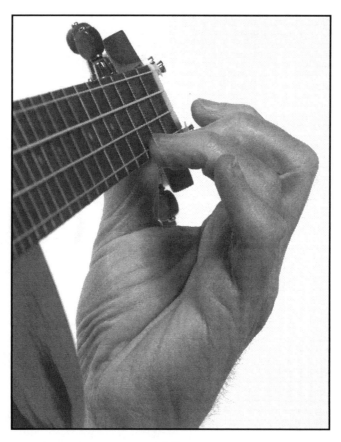

# Section 2
# The Songs

For Online Video & Audio Access, go to this address on the internet:

cvls.com/extras/kidsuke

# He's Got the Whole World
# Chords & Strum

We're ready for our first real song. We're using the C and G chords we just learned and strumming twice per line.

The strum markers match up with the words to the song that you sing at the same time. So for the first line, you would strum while you sing "whole" and then again with "in his".

He's got the whole          world          in  his          hands  he's got the

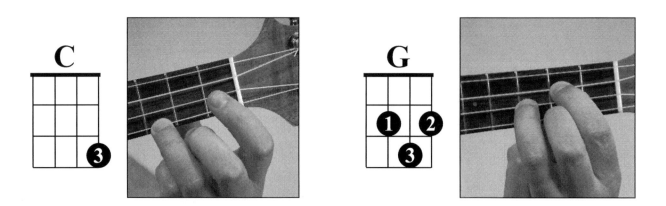

# He's Got the Whole World

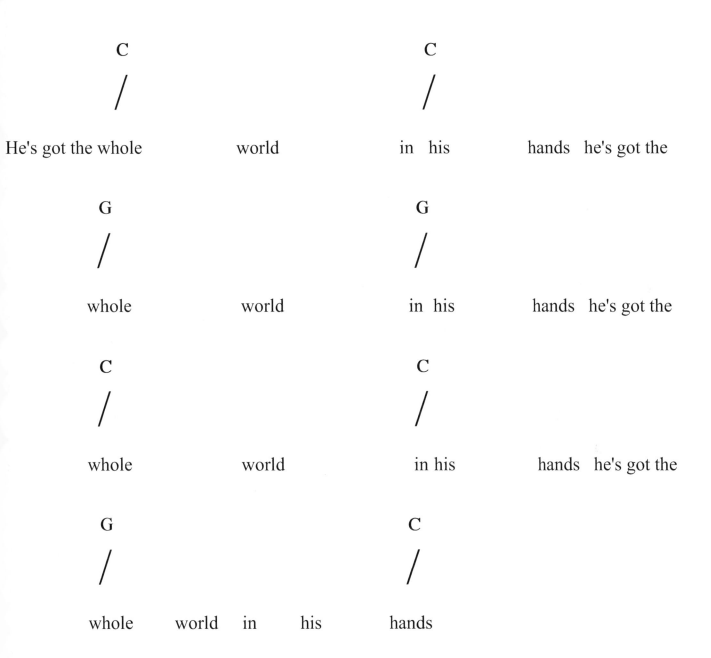

```
   C                        C
   /                        /
He's got the whole  world    in  his      hands   he's got the

   G                        G
   /                        /
   whole       world         in  his      hands   he's got the

   C                        C
   /                        /
   whole       world         in his       hands   he's got the

   G                        C
   /                        /
   whole    world  in    his      hands
```

Watch and listen to the video instruction to make sure you're playing correctly.
You can access the video by going to this address on the internet:

cvls.com/extras/kidsuke

# Mary Had a Little Lamb
## Chords & Strum

Let's try using the same chords and strum idea with a new song.

C                                            C

/                                           /

1        2        3        4        1        2        3        4

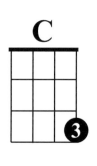

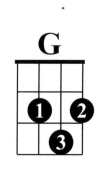

# Mary Had a Little Lamb

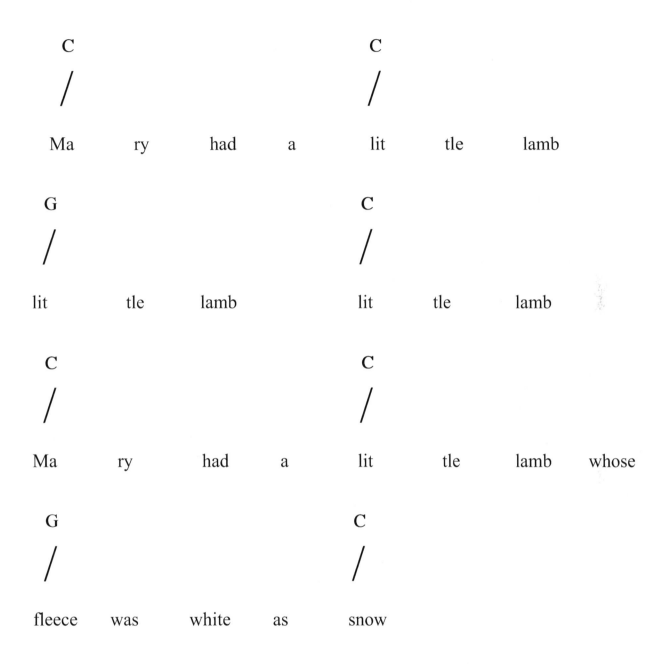

C                                     C

/                                   /

Ma    ry    had    a    lit    tle    lamb

G                                       C

/                                   /

lit    tle    lamb       lit    tle    lamb

C                                       C

/                                   /

Ma    ry    had    a    lit    tle    lamb    whose

G                                       C

/                                   /

fleece    was    white    as    snow

# Wheels On the Bus
## Chords & Strum

We're now going to strum four times for each line of the song.

C

/       /       /       /

1     2     3     4     1     2     3     4

Up to this point, we've shown which chord to play for every strum. Now that we're adding more strums, we'll continue to play the same chord until it changes.

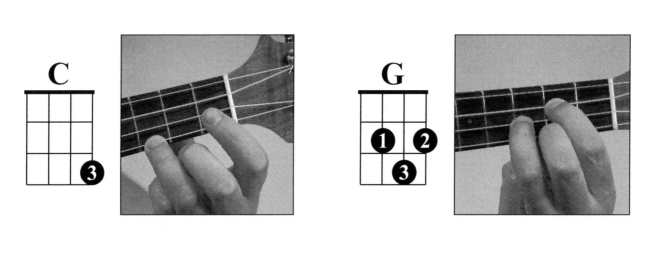

# Wheels On the Bus

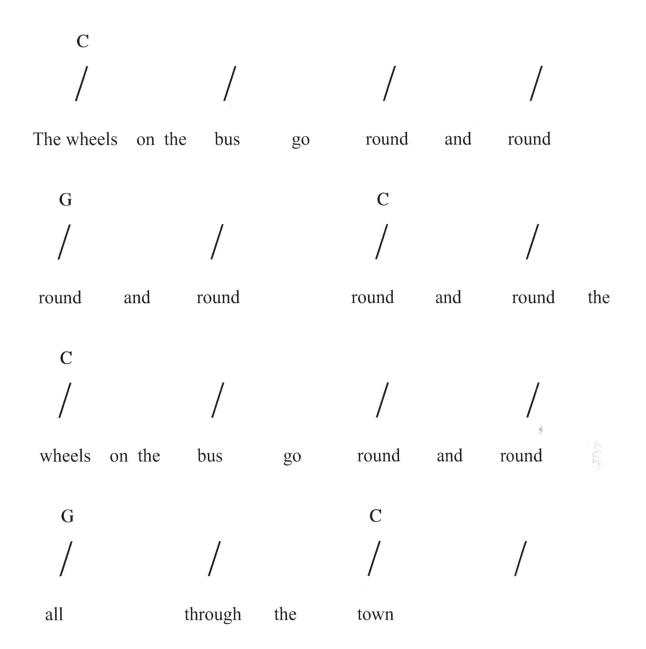

C
/      /      /      /

The wheels   on the   bus   go   round   and   round

G                  C
/      /      /      /

round   and   round     round   and   round   the

C
/      /      /      /

wheels   on the   bus   go   round   and   round

G                  C
/      /      /      /

all      through   the   town

# Row, Row, Row Your Boat
## Chords & Strum

For this song, you'll have to switch between the C and G chord a little quicker with your left hand.

C

/       /       /       /

1    2    3    4     1    2    3    4

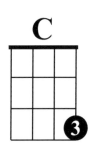
C

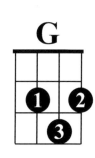
G

26

# Row, Row, Row Your Boat

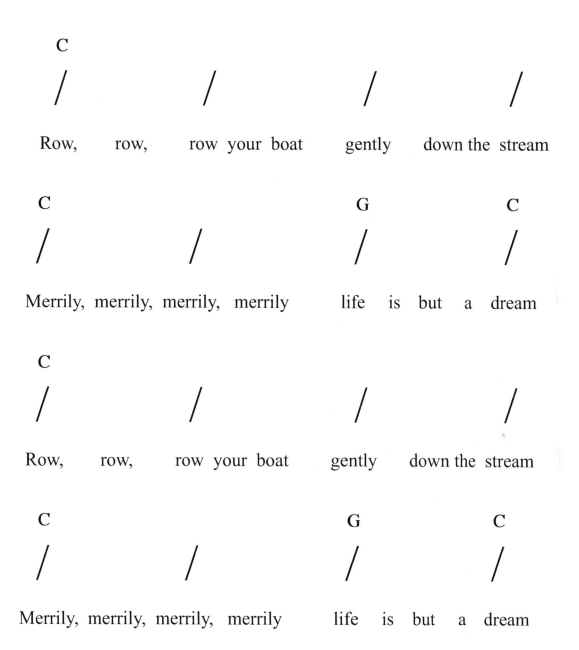

C
/ / / /

Row, row, row your boat gently down the stream

C G C
/ / / /

Merrily, merrily, merrily, merrily life is but a dream

C
/ / / /

Row, row, row your boat gently down the stream

C G C
/ / / /

Merrily, merrily, merrily, merrily life is but a dream

# Hush Little Baby
## Chords & Strum

It's time to learn a new chord. This chord is called a $G^7$.

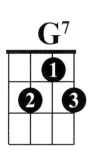

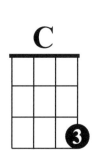

Try practicing this switch.

| C | $G^7$ | C | $G^7$ | C | $G^7$ | C | $G^7$ |
|---|---|---|---|---|---|---|---|
| / | / | / | / | / | / | / | / |
| 1 | 2 | 3 | 4 | 1 | 2 | 3 | 4 |

In the song, we'll strum twice per line.

| C | | | | $G^7$ | | | |
|---|---|---|---|---|---|---|---|
| / | | | | / | | | |
| 1 | 2 | 3 | 4 | 1 | 2 | 3 | 4 |

# Hush Little Baby

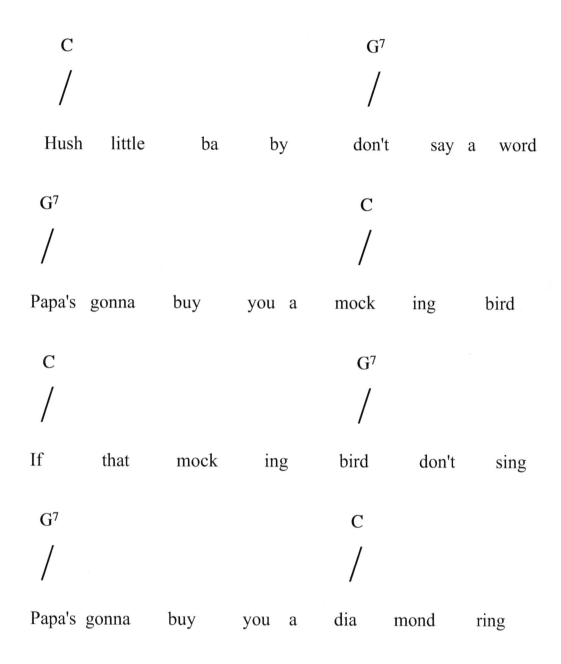

C

G⁷

Hush    little    ba    by    don't    say   a    word

G⁷

C

Papa's gonna    buy    you   a    mock    ing    bird

C

G⁷

If    that    mock    ing    bird    don't    sing

G⁷

C

Papa's gonna    buy    you   a    dia    mond    ring

# Rain, Rain, Go Away
## Chords & Strum

Let's use C and G7 again in a new song. This time we'll play four strums per line.

C

1     2     3     4     1     2     3     4

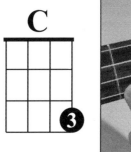
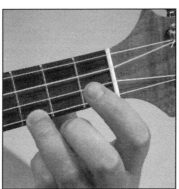
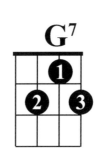

# Rain, Rain, Go Away

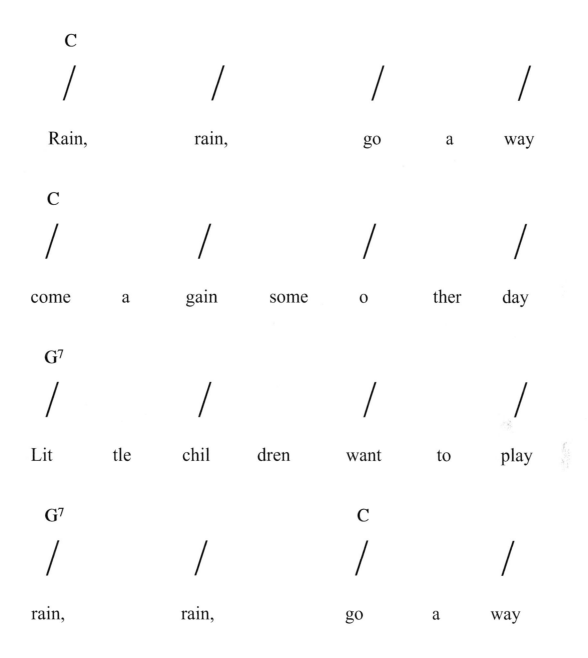

C
/      /      /      /

Rain,      rain,      go   a   way

C
/      /      /      /

come   a   gain   some   o   ther   day

G$^7$
/      /      /      /

Lit   tle   chil   dren   want   to   play

G$^7$                C
/      /      /      /

rain,      rain,      go   a   way

# Hokey Pokey
## Chords & Strum

We'll play four strums per line with the C and G7 chords.

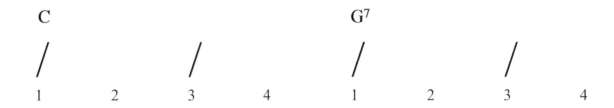

C                              G⁷

/        /        /        /        /        /

1      2      3      4      1      2      3      4

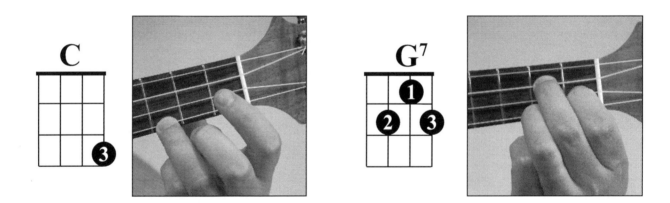

# Hokey Pokey

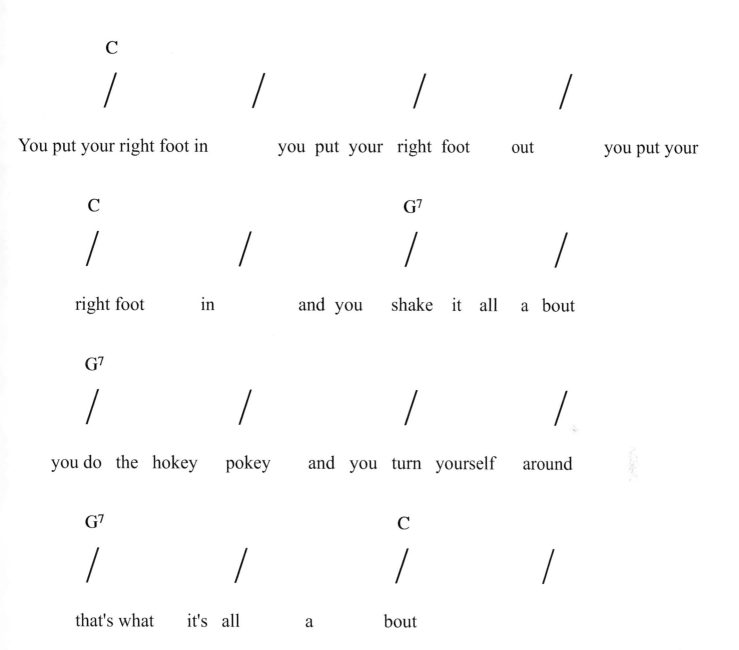

C
/      /      /      /

You put your right foot in      you put your right foot out      you put your

C                  G⁷
/      /      /      /

right foot     in      and you   shake it all a bout

G⁷
/      /      /      /

you do the hokey   pokey    and you turn yourself   around

G⁷                 C
/      /      /      /

that's what   it's all     a      bout

# If You're Happy and You Know It
## Chords & Strum

It's time to learn a new chord. The F chord uses two fingers.

**F**

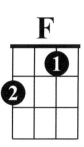

Practice playing each string, one at a time. Is each note clear? Or do you hear a buzz or soft note? You may need to arch your fingers more to get a clear sound. Once you can play it clearly, practice switching between the C and F chords.

| C | F | C | F | C | F | C | F |
|---|---|---|---|---|---|---|---|
| / | / | / | / | / | / | / | / |
| 1 | 2 | 3 | 4 | 1 | 2 | 3 | 4 |

We'll play two strums per line for this song.

| C | | | | F | | | |
|---|---|---|---|---|---|---|---|
| / | | | | / | | | |
| 1 | 2 | 3 | 4 | 1 | 2 | 3 | 4 |

**C**

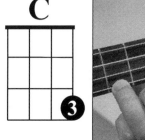

**F**

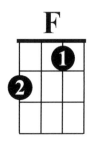

**G**

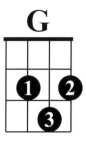

# If You're Happy and You Know It

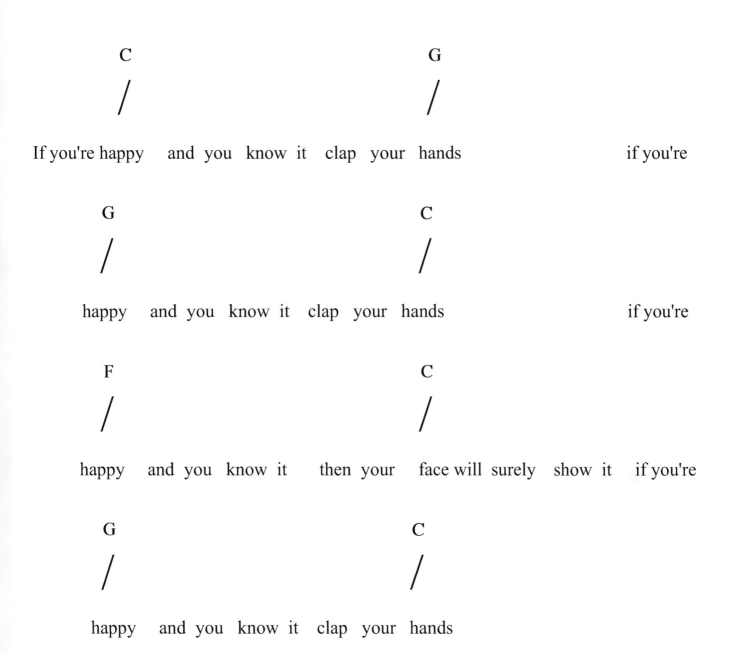

C                                               G

If you're happy    and   you   know   it   clap   your   hands             if you're

G                                               C

happy    and   you   know   it   clap   your   hands             if you're

F                                               C

happy    and   you   know   it     then   your    face will   surely    show   it    if you're

G                                               C

happy    and   you   know   it   clap   your   hands

# Itsy Bitsy Spider
# Chords & Strum

We'll strum four times per line in the next song. The chord changes chords will be a bit faster so you may need to practice this very slowly.

| C | | | G | | C | |
|---|---|---|---|---|---|---|
| / | / | | / | | / | |
| 1 | 2 | 3 | 4 | 1 | 2 | 3 | 4 |

Let's use the C, F, and G chords again in this song.

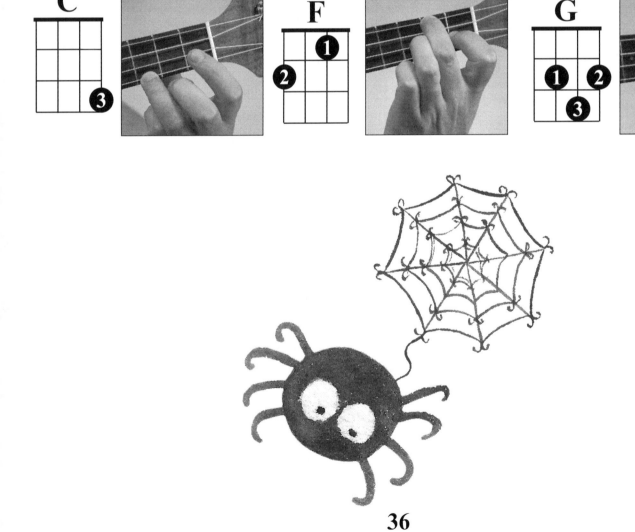

# Itsy Bitsy Spider

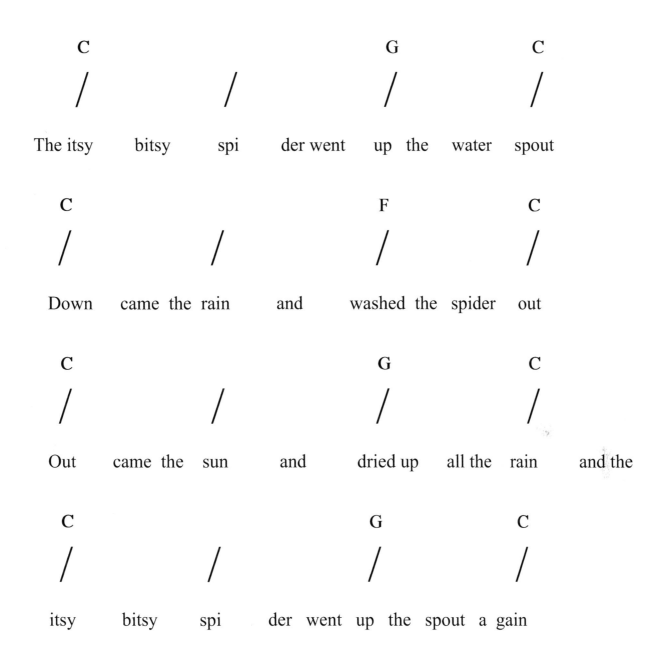

C / / G / C /

The itsy    bitsy    spi    der went    up the    water    spout

C / / F / C /

Down    came the rain    and    washed the    spider    out

C / / G / C /

Out    came the    sun    and    dried up    all the    rain    and the

C / / G / C /

itsy    bitsy    spi    der went up the    spout a gain

# John Jacob Jingleheimer Schmidt
## Chords & Strum

We'll use the same three chords, C, F, and G, but this is the first time we switch from F to G. Let's practice that.

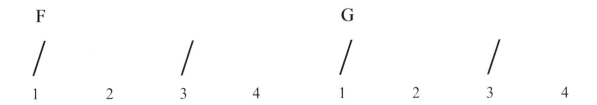

F                              G

/           /           /           /

1        2        3        4        1        2        3        4

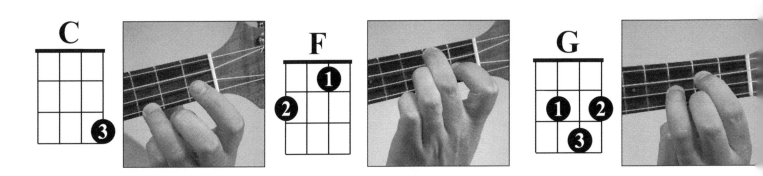

We'll strum down four times per line.

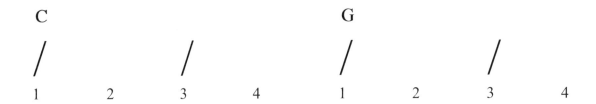

C                              G

/           /           /           /

1        2        3        4        1        2        3        4

# John Jacob Jingleheimer Schmidt

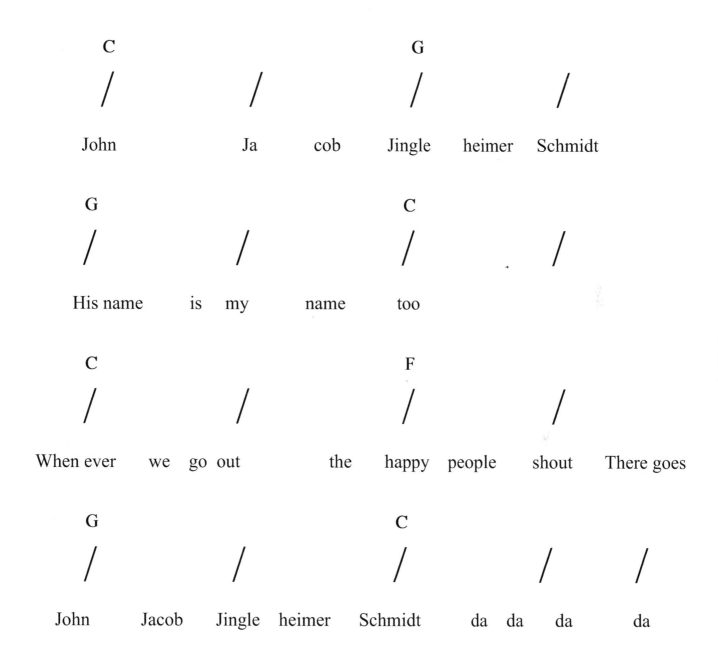

# Oh When the Saints
## Chords & Strum

We'll strum four times per line in the next song.

C

/       /       /       /

1     2     3     4     1     2     3     4

We'll use the C, F, and G chords again.

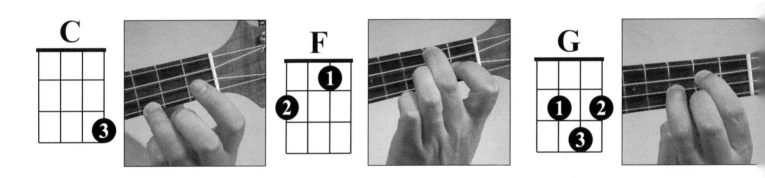

# Oh When the Saints

C
/       /       /       /

Oh when the Saints             go    march    ing

C
/       /       /       /

in            oh    when    the

C
/       /       /       /

Saints      go      march      ing

G
/       /       /       /

in           Oh    how    I

C
/       /       /       /

want      to      be      in    that

F
/       /       /       /

num    ber          Oh    when    the

C                      G
/       /       /       /

Saints      go      march      ing

C
/       /       /       /

in

# Twinkle Twinkle Little Star
## Chords & Strum

We'll strum eight times per line in the next song.

C                                    F            C

/      /      /      /      /      /      /      /

1      2      3      4      1      2      3      4

Once again, we'll use the C, F, and G chords.

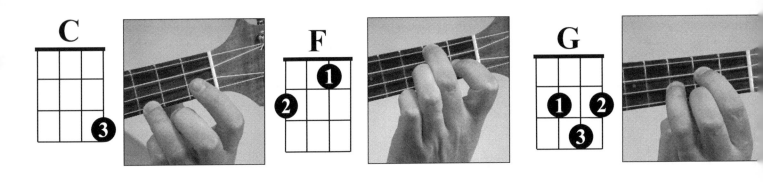

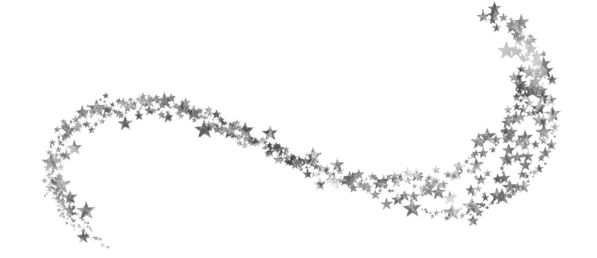

# Twinkle Twinkle Little Star

| C | | | | F | | C | |
|---|---|---|---|---|---|---|---|
| / | / | / | / | / | / | / | / |
| Twin | kle | twin | kle | lit | tle | star | |

| F | | C | | G | | C | |
|---|---|---|---|---|---|---|---|
| / | / | / | / | / | / | / | / |
| how | I | won | der | what | you | are | |

| C | | F | | C | | G | |
|---|---|---|---|---|---|---|---|
| / | / | / | / | / | / | / | / |
| high | a | bove | the | world | so | high | |

| C | | F | | C | | G | |
|---|---|---|---|---|---|---|---|
| / | / | / | / | / | / | / | / |
| like | a | dia | mond | in | the | sky | |

| C | | | | F | | C | |
|---|---|---|---|---|---|---|---|
| / | / | / | / | / | / | / | / |
| Twin | kle | twin | kle | lit | tle | star | |

| F | | C | | G | | C | |
|---|---|---|---|---|---|---|---|
| / | / | / | / | / | / | / | / |
| how | I | won | der | what | you | are | |

# Appendix

# Common Chords

On the following pages, you will find a chart of commonly used chords you will need to advance your playing and learn more songs. There are a couple of new techniques you'll need to learn.

## The Bar

This is a bar and means to bar your index finger over the 3rd, 2nd, and 1st strings.

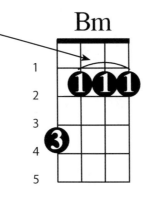

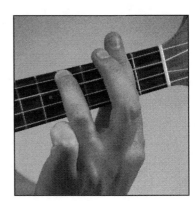

## Moving Up The Neck

Notice that the fret numbers have changed and you are starting at the 4th fret.

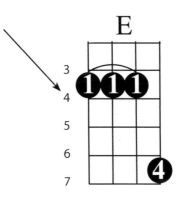

# Common Chords

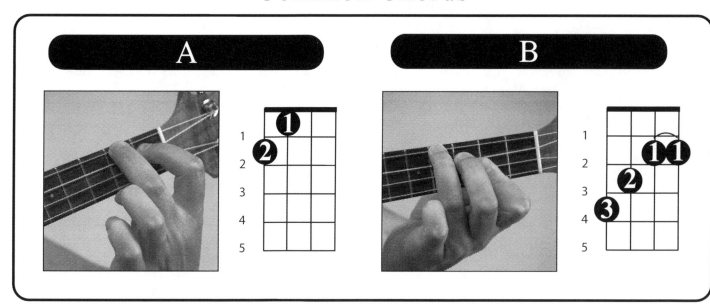

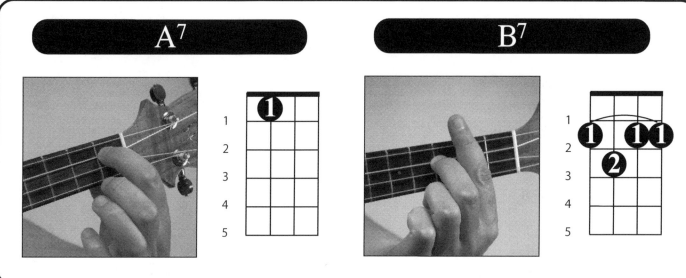

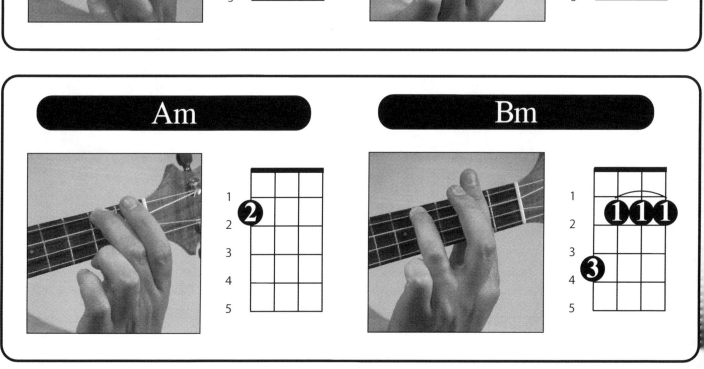

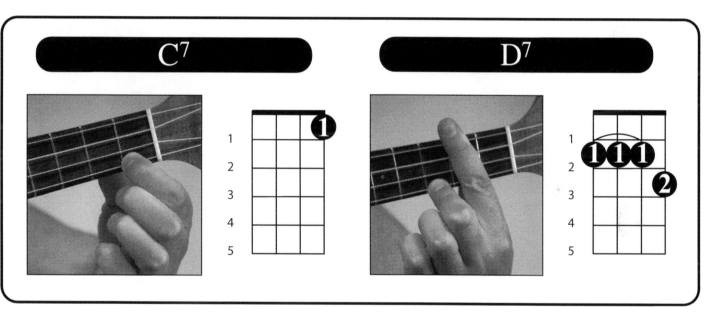

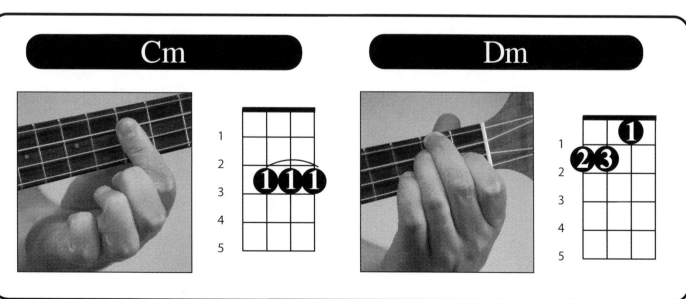

47

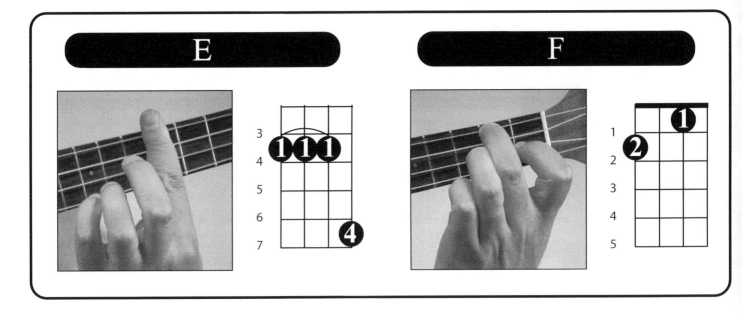

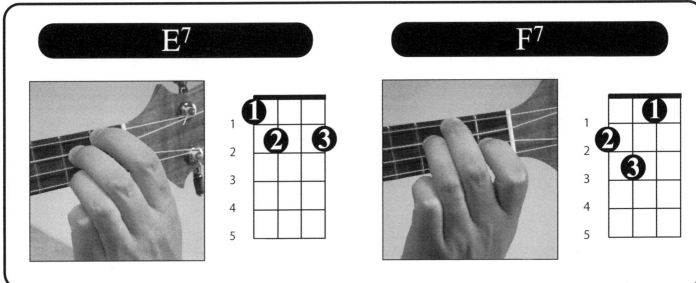

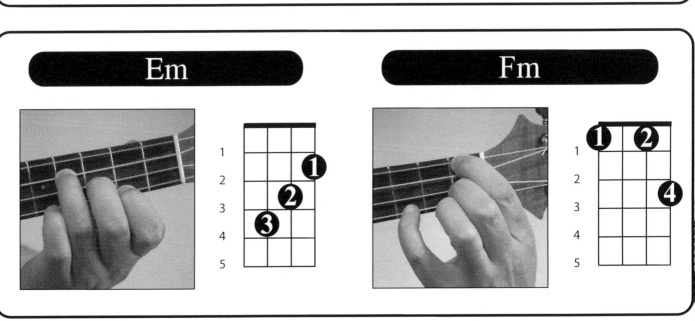

48

## G

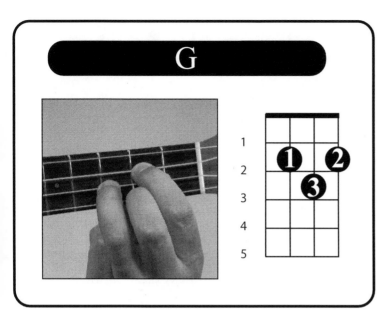

## G⁷

## Gm

49

# Beginner Series for Kids

Watch & Learn, Inc. has other products for elementary school-aged children. These can be used with this course or on its own.

Designed to quickly teach the beginning student to play songs they will know and love. These lessons start by playing with just the right hand and gradually build to adding the left hand thumb and learning how to play with both hands. Song arrangements provide an easy transition from learning the basics to covering more interesting rhythms, techniques, and musical ideas. The book features standard music notation for each song and exercise along with fingering notation and hand shifts to make the course easier to learn. This method includes online access to over an hour of video instruction that will help the child play with proper form and timing. The combination of book, video, and audio make this the easiest to understand piano course for kids available.

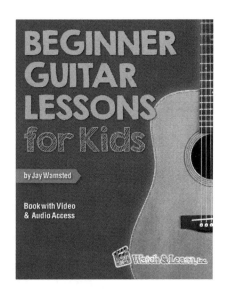

Designed to help the absolute beginning student learn to play the guitar. This step-by-step course is designed for elementary school-aged children (ages 5-10) and quickly teaches the student to play songs they will know and love. These lessons start by playing beginner chord shapes (G, C, G7, D) that are easier for younger students with smaller hands. Song arrangements and strum patterns were carefully selected to help children have early success playing the guitar. This course will help the young beginner avoid getting frustrated and quitting the instrument.

The next section of the book teaches the same songs but with full chord shapes. This can be used for either a beginner with larger hands or for a student who is now ready to expand their playing. This course includes online access to video instruction and audio tracks. The video lessons allow the child to hear and see how each song is played from a rhythm and technique standpoint. The video also shows the guitar, both hands, and the sheet music on-screen at the same time.

# Follow-up Products

These Watch & Learn products are also available and would be the next step beyond this course.

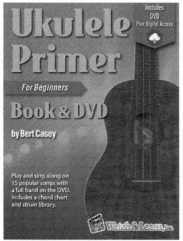

Designed to help the beginner learn how to play the ukulele. This course can be used with a Soprano, Concert, or Tenor ukulele. This lesson starts off with the absolute basics like parts of the ukulele, tuning (G, C, E, A), left and right hand position, and how to strum. You will learn how to play chords and different strum patterns in the context of fifteen popular songs. The book contains written instruction, music notation, helpful tips, chord charts, and detailed photographs. The video provides ninety minutes of instruction for all of the techniques and songs covered in the book. This is the perfect course for teaching a beginner how to play the ukulele.

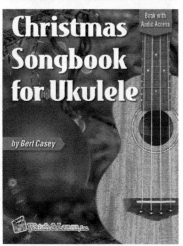

Features beginner to intermediate arrangements for classic Christmas songs. Each song features detailed strum patterns, chord charts, lyrics, and vocal melody notation. The songs were arranged so that you can play the rhythm part while singing along. The second portion of this book displays each song along with extended lyrics and chord progressions. This is a great setup for sing-alongs because the lyrics are written in a large font so that multiple singers and musicians can read along. This course also includes online access to audio tracks to help you learn and practice.

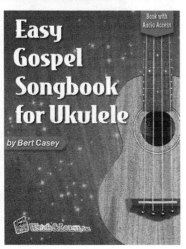

Features beginner to intermediate arrangements for classic gospel songs. Each song features detailed strum patterns, chord charts, lyrics, and vocal melody notation. The songs were arranged so that you can play the rhythm part while singing along. The second portion of this book displays each song along with extended lyrics and chord progressions. This is a great setup for sing-alongs because the lyrics are written in a large font so that multiple singers and musicians can read along. This course also includes online access to audio tracks to help you learn and practice. playing along with other instruments.

All of these products are available at Amazon.com.

Made in United States
Orlando, FL
06 February 2025